The Trial of Aar

GW01159490

Joseph P. Brady

Alpha Editions

This edition published in 2024

ISBN : 9789362094988

Design and Setting By
Alpha Editions
www.alphaedis.com
Email - info@alphaedis.com

Contents

PREFACE...- 1 -

THE TRIAL OF AARON BURR...- 2 -

PREFACE

Among the records of the United States Courts at Richmond, Virginia, are the original papers in the case of the "United States versus Aaron Burr, Indictment for Treason." The tawny fingers of time have dealt gently with these papers, and although more than a century old they are still in a good state of preservation.

The story of the trial of Aaron Burr has often been written, and there is little new that can be added; but these old manuscripts and official documents, so historic in their character, should at least in some form survive the ravages of time. It is with this thought in mind, and with the hope that possibly some fact not already recorded in history might be disclosed by the original papers, that this brief history is written.

THE TRIAL OF AARON BURR

On the evening of the 26th of March, 1807, Aaron Burr, attended by a military guard of nine men, under the command of Major Nicholas Perkins, who had been largely instrumental in his arrest, arrived in the City of Richmond, Virginia. Immediately upon his arrival he was lodged in the Eagle Tavern, the leading hostelry of its time in that city, where he remained confined until March 30th, when he was delivered to the civil authorities by virtue of a warrant issued by Chief Justice Marshall.

The preliminary examination of Burr was private. The warrant was served on him in his apartment by Major Scott, the Marshal of the Virginia District, who, after informing him of the object of his visit, conducted him to another room, where he was brought before the Chief Justice. The few persons present were Cæsar A. Rodney, Attorney-General of the United States; George Hay, the United States Attorney for the Virginia District; Edmund Randolph and John Wickham, counsel for the prisoner; the United States Marshal and his two deputies; and a few friends of the counsel for Burr.

The evidence introduced on behalf of the prosecution was a copy of the record in the case of Bollman and Swartout in the Supreme Court of the United States, which contained the depositions of General Eaton and General Wilkinson directly connecting Burr with the offense charged against him. No verbal testimony was heard, except that of Major Perkins, who told of the arrest of the prisoner and of his conveyance of him to Richmond.

At the conclusion of the evidence a motion in writing was submitted by Mr. Hay for the commitment of the accused on two charges, viz:—

First. For a high misdemeanor, in setting on foot, within the United States, a military expedition against the dominions of the King of Spain, a foreign prince, with whom the United States, at the time of the offense, were, and still are, at peace.

Second. For treason in assembling an armed force, with a design to seize the city of New Orleans, to revolutionize the territory attached to it, and to separate the western from the Atlantic states.

It soon developed that this motion would cause considerable discussion, and as previously agreed upon by counsel, with the approval of the Chief Justice, the further hearing of the case was adjourned to the House of Delegates in the Capitol, where all subsequent proceedings were had.

The argument on the motion lasted two days. It was opened by Mr. Hay for the United States. He was followed by Mr. Wickham and Mr. Randolph for the accused. Colonel Burr spoke about ten minutes in his own behalf, and Mr. Rodney, the Attorney-General of the United States, closed the discussion.

The third day of the trial, the Chief Justice delivered his written opinion. "On an application of this kind," says he, "I certainly should not require that proof which would be necessary to convict the person to be committed on a trial in chief; nor should I even require that which should absolutely convince my own mind of the guilt of the accused; but I ought to require, and I should require, that probable cause be shown; and I understand probable cause to be a case made out by proof furnishing good reason to believe that the crime alleged has been committed by the person charged with having committed it." The Chief Justice then reviews the testimony of General Eaton and General Wilkinson in the Swartout and Bollman case to show how far these charges are supported by probable cause, and in conclusion delivers himself as follows: "I shall not therefore insert in the commitment the charge of high treason, since it will be entirely in the power of the Attorney-General to prefer an indictment against the prisoner for high treason should he be furnished with the necessary testimony."

Burr was now called upon to give bond, and the amount to be required of him gave rise to much discussion. The Chief Justice stated, "that he wished it to be neither too large to amount to oppression, nor too small to defeat the objects of justice." It had occurred to him that the sum of ten thousand dollars would perhaps avoid both these extremes. Mr. Hay earnestly insisted upon a larger amount, but the amount was fixed at ten thousand. Burr was then bailed for his appearance at the next term of the Circuit Court of the United States to convene at Richmond on the 22d of May next, to answer the charge of high misdemeanor.

Aaron Burr was now at liberty. President Jefferson was enraged at the result of the first trial. The feeling between the partisans of the Administration and the Federalists, to which political party Marshall belonged, was rampant. The friends of Jefferson charged Marshall with having permitted his political bias and personal dislike of the President to warp his judgment in favor of Burr throughout the trial, and Jefferson in one of his letters to Senator Giles, written a few days after Burr's first examination at Richmond, refers to the *tricks* of the judges in hastening the trial so as to clear Burr. It was evident that Jefferson was to be the real prosecutor of Burr, and had made up his mind to convict him at whatever cost.

The 22d of May, 1807, the United States Circuit Court for the Virginia District convened in the House of Delegates in the City of Richmond, Virginia, with Chief Justice Marshall and Cyrus Griffin, District Judge, on the bench.

Long before the hour the Court was to meet the hall and the entrances to the Capitol were thronged with people. Not a few of them were witnesses and persons summoned as grand jurors, while others were attracted by the notoriety of the trial. There could be seen John Randolph, of Roanoke, "the brilliant, eccentric leader of the Quids," in the House, and afterwards United States Senator from Virginia; Andrew Jackson, who was loud in his denunciation of Jefferson and his administration for "persecuting his innocent friend"; Winfield Scott, then a young lawyer just admitted to practice; General Eaton, with a grudge against the Government for its failure to pay his claim for services and cash advanced while consul in Barbary, and with whom Burr had talked with great freedom about his plans; Commodore Truxton, another disgruntled officer of the Government in whom Burr had confided; Col. Morgan, a valiant old campaigner from the West, and his two stalwart sons, whose services Burr tried to enlist, but whom Jefferson credited with giving him the first intimation of Burr's designs; John Graham, who had been sent out by the Administration to the Mississippi territory as its confidential agent to circumvent Burr and expose the conspiracy; Colonel Dupiester, one of the leading spirits in the plot and Burr's trusted friend and ally; Jonathan Dayton, formerly speaker of the House of Representatives and Ex-Senator from the State of New Jersey, and John Smith, lately a Senator from Ohio, both friends of Burr and prominent in the conspiracy with him;

Dr. Erick Bollman, an educated German, who had recently distinguished himself by a gallant but unsuccessful attempt to rescue Lafayette from prison in the castle of Olmutz, Austria, and in whom Burr had confided. Jefferson expected Bollman to give testimony that might criminate himself, and during the trial sent through District Attorney Hay a pardon for him, which Bollman indignantly refused to accept. And thither also came Governor Alston of South Carolina, and his wife, the beautiful and accomplished Theodosia, the only daughter of Aaron Burr; who had fled to his side the moment she had heard of his arrest.

The court was formally opened at half past twelve o'clock, and probably there never was such an array of learning and legal attainments as was present on that occasion. Foremost and overshadowing all was John Marshall, the Chief Justice. "Gentlemen of the profession," said Parton, "who witnessed the trial, who saw the effective dignity with which the judge presided over the court, who heard him read those opinions, so elaborate and right, though necessarily prepared on the spur of the moment, regarded it as the finest display of judicial skill and judicial rectitude which they had ever beheld."

Seated at the bar and appearing in behalf of the United States were Colonel George Hay, William Wirt and Alexander MacRae.

Colonel Hay was a son-in-law of James Monroe, who was afterwards President of the United States. He was a lawyer of great industry and much ability, and bore the laboring oar in the trial. He was a zealous partisan of Jefferson, and was assisted in the prosecution by almost daily communications from him. Later he was appointed United States judge for the Virginia district. Mr. Wirt was present at the personal request of President Jefferson. He was the most eloquent and accomplished advocate then at the Richmond bar. There was no one whose rising to speak "so instantaneously hushed the spectators to silence." "A handsome, fortunate, brilliant, high-minded man was William Wirt," says Parton, "the toil of whose life it was to achieve those solid attainments which alone make brilliancy of utterance endurable in a court of justice." Mr. MacRae, the third attorney for the government, was then Lieutenant-Governor of Virginia, and while less able than his two colleagues, was a lawyer of "respectable ability and a sharp tongue."

On the side of the defense were the greatest lawyers of the time. The best known of them was perhaps Edmund Randolph. Mr. Randolph had been a delegate to the Continental Congress and to the Philadelphia Constitutional Convention, Attorney-General and Governor of Virginia, and Attorney-General and Secretary of State under Washington. He was a man of great experience and learning. Associated with him from the day of Burr's arrival in Richmond was John Wickham, grandfather of the late General W. C. Wickham and great-grandfather of Hon. Henry T. Wickham, an eminent member of the present bar of Virginia. Mr. Wickham was regarded by many as the ablest lawyer at the Virginia bar. "The qualities," says Mr. William Wirt in the *British Spy*, "by which Mr. Wickham strikes the multitude are his ingenuity and his wit. But those who look more closely into the anatomy of his mind, disclose many properties of much higher dignity and importance. This gentleman, in my opinion, unites in himself a greater diversity of talents and acquirements than any other at the bar in Virginia." Another great lawyer of counsel for Burr, and probably the greatest one of his day, was Luther Martin of Maryland. He and Burr had formed a friendship about two years before in Washington, when Justice Chase of the Supreme Court of the United States was impeached by the House of Representatives and tried by the Senate for abuse of his office in certain political trials. Burr was then Vice-President of the United States, and presided over the Senate in that celebrated proceeding, says a contemporary, "with the dignity and impartiality of an angel, but with the rigor of a devil." Martin was the leading counsel for Justice Chase, and greatly distinguished himself. Conspicuous also was Benjamin Botts, father of the distinguished John Minor Botts, who although the youngest man on the side of the defense, had already become eminent in his profession.

The other counsel for Burr were Charles Lee, an Ex-Attorney-General of the United States, and a lawyer of much learning; "Jack" Baker, who was more of a "good fellow" than lawyer; and Washington Irving, then attracting some attention in the field of letters, who to use his own words, "went to Richmond on an informal retainer from one of the friends of Col. Burr," although, as he said, "his client had little belief in his legal erudition, and did not look for any approach to a professional debut, but thought he might in some way or other be of service with his pen."

But of the defense *facile princeps* was Burr himself. He was keenly alive to every proceeding, and while the burden fell upon others, no move was made, or point conceded, without his sanction. Mr. Robertson, the reporter of the trial, says: "Among these stood Aaron Burr, proudly pre-eminent in point of intelligence to his brethren of the bar, who had been vice-president of the United States, and now accused of the highest and darkest crime in the criminal code. Standing before the Supreme tribunal of his country, and with the eyes of the nation upon him, he was, in the opinion of many, already condemned. He had the talent and tact, and the resources of the Government to contend against, and every faculty of his mind was exerted in his own defense. The magnitude of the charge, the number of persons involved, the former high standing and extraordinary fortunes of the accused, had excited an interest in the community such as never before had been known."

WARRANT FOR ARREST OF BURR

The Marshal had summoned for service on the grand jury the most intelligent and representative citizens of the Commonwealth. Prominent among them was William B. Giles. He had served in both branches of the Legislature of

Virginia; had been Governor of the State of Virginia; and representative and senator in the Congress of the United States. Senator Giles was a partisan of Jefferson, a member of what John Randolph called "the President's back-stair cabinet." He was the leader of the republicans in the Senate, and had been foremost in the assaults on the "last stronghold of Federalism—the Judiciary."

When Senator Giles was called on the *voir dire* he was challenged personally by Burr. Burr claimed the same right of challenging grand jurors for favor that he had of challenging petit jurors, and was sustained in his position by the Chief Justice. His objection to Giles was that, on occasions in the Senate, he had pronounced his opinion on certain documents sent to that body by President Jefferson attributing to Burr treasonable designs, and upon such information advocating the suspension of the writ of *habeas corpus*. He stated that he could produce evidence, if necessary, of public utterances of Senator Giles confirming these views. Senator Giles was stricken from the panel.

Another former United States Senator, and afterwards Governor of Virginia, summoned as a grand juror, was Wilson Cary Nicholas. He was a personal enemy of Burr, and when his name was called Burr challenged him. Colonel Nicholas had served three years in the Senate when Burr presided over it, and had taken a very decided part in favor of the election of his successor. He had freely expressed his suspicions, both in correspondence and publicly, of Colonel Burr's probable objects in the west. He was rejected.

Some of the other distinguished citizens of Virginia summoned by the Marshal, and who served on the grand jury, were Littleton Waller Tazewell and James Pleasants, both afterwards United States Senators and Governors of Virginia; Joseph C. Cabell, one of the founders with Jefferson of the University of Virginia; William Daniel, father of the late Judge William Daniel of the Court of Appeals of Virginia, and grandfather of John Warwick Daniel, the lamented senator from Virginia; and Colonel James Barbour, afterwards Governor of Virginia, United States Senator, Secretary of War under John Quincy Adams, and Minister to England.

The general belief in the guilt of the accused was manifested at the very beginning of the trial. The proclamations and the special messages of President Jefferson to Congress, and the depositions of Generals Eaton and Wilkinson had had their effect on the public mind. A number of citizens summoned for service on the grand jury frankly admitted they had prejudged the case, and in consequence of such disqualifications and excuses the original panel was reduced to fourteen.

The court, being now without a legal grand jury in attendance, directed the Marshal to summon from the bystanders two additional persons. The Marshal summoned and returned John Randolph and William Foushee. Mr. Randolph was named as foreman, but upon being asked to take the oath, requested to be excused from serving. He had formed an opinion concerning the nature and tendency of certain transactions imputed to Mr. Burr. He had a strong prepossession, but thought he could divest himself of it upon evidence. Mr. Burr observed that he was afraid they would be unable to find any man without this prepossession. "The rule is," said the Chief Justice, "that a man must not only have formed, but declared an opinion, in order to exclude him from serving on the jury." Mr. Randolph replied that he had no recollection of having declared one, and he was thereupon sworn as foreman.

Dr. Foushee when called to be sworn was found to be disqualified, and was permitted to withdraw. Colonel James Barbour was called in his stead and accepted.

The selection of the grand jury having been completed, the grand jury was duly sworn by the clerk. It was composed of the following citizens:

John Randolph, Foreman, Joseph Eggleston, Joseph C. Cabell, Littleton W. Tazewell, Robert Taylor, James Pleasants, John Brockenbrough, William Daniel, James M. Garnett, John Mercer, Edward Pegram, Munford Beverly, John Ambler, Thomas Harrison, Alexander Shephard and James Barbour.

The Chief Justice promptly delivered an appropriate charge to the grand jury. He dwelt more particularly upon the definition and nature of treason, and the testimony requisite to prove it. He said in part: "To you by the Constitution and laws of our country is confided the important right of accusing those whose offenses shall have rendered them subject to punishment under the laws of the United States. It is on you that the fundamental principles on which the stability of our political institutions and the safety of individuals most greatly depend. For to little purpose would laws be formed to protect the innocent of the body politic from crimes of the worst nature if a misplaced nonentity should control the execution of them. Juries, gentlemen, as well as judges, should be superior to every temptation, which hope, fear or compassion, may suggest; who will allow no influence to balance their love of justice; who will follow no guide but the laws of their country.

"In outlining to you, gentlemen of the jury, those offenses which are cognizable in the court, and which may scarcely be noticed by you, the first on the calendar, as well as the highest known atrocity, is treason against the United States. With a jealousy peculiar to themselves the American people have withdrawn the subject from the power of their legislature, and have declared in their Constitution that 'treason against the United States shall consist only in levying war against them, or in adhering to their enemies, giving them aid and comfort.'"

After the grand jury had retired Colonel Burr addressed the court on the propriety of specially instructing them in regard to the admissibility of certain evidence, which he stated would be laid before the grand jury by the attorney for the United States. Mr. Hay opposed this application. He said he could never agree to it, and he trusted the court also would never sanction such a suggestion; that Colonel Burr stood before the court on the same footing as any other citizen, and he hoped the court would not distinguish between his case and that of any other. The question was postponed for further discussion. The court then adjourned to the following morning.

The court met the next day and the grand jury also appeared. It became apparent that nothing effectual could be done until the arrival of General Wilkinson, the most important witness for the Government. The grand jury were therefore adjourned from day to day until he put in his appearance.

Meanwhile Mr. Hay had moved to commit Burr on a charge of high treason against the United States. On his preliminary examination he was bailed on the charge of misdemeanor, but said Mr. Hay "there was no evidence of an overt act. The evidence is different now."

This motion was discussed at length throughout the day, and provoked one of the most eloquent debates of the whole trial and revealed the political passions of the day. Mr. Botts "begged leave to make a few remarks on this extraordinary application, and the pernicious effects such an extraordinary measure, if generally practised, would inevitably produce. The organ particularly appropriated for the consideration of the evidence which the motion calls for, is the grand jury; and the motion is to divest the grand jury of the office, which the Constitution and laws have appropriated to them, and to devolve it upon the court. The grand juror's oath is to inquire into all crimes and misdemeanors committed within the district of the State of which they are freeholders. Their office is to perform that which the court is now called upon to perform. To them belongs the exclusive duty of inquiring and examining into all species of evidence, which may lead to a conviction of the crimes of which Colonel Burr is now charged; but there is a great objection to the exercise of this examining and committing power by a high law officer, who is to preside upon the trial, when the grand jury, the appropriate tribunal, is in session."

After Mr. Botts had taken his seat, Mr. Hay in response to an inquiry by the Chief Justice, as to whether the counsel for the prosecution intended to open the case more fully, stated, "that he had not intended to open it more fully; he did not himself entertain the least doubt, that if there was sufficient proof produced to justify the commitment of Colonel Burr, the court had completely the right to commit him."

Mr. Wickham complained because the gentlemen on the other side had not given them notice of their intended motion. "We come into this discussion completely off our guard, completely unprepared." "The fact is this," replied Mr. Hay, "Mr. Wilkinson is known to be a material witness in this prosecution; his arrival in Virginia, might be announced in this city, before he himself reached it. I do not intend to say what effect it might produce upon Colonel Burr's mind; but certainly Colonel Burr would be able to effect his escape, merely upon paying the recognizance of his present bail. My only object then was to keep his person safe, until we could have investigated the charge of treason; and I really did not know but that if Colonel Burr had been previously apprised of my motion he might have attempted to avoid it. But I did not promise to make the communication to the opposite counsel, because it might have defeated the very end for which it was intended."

Mr. Wickham observed, "that the present motion was unprecedented in a system of criminal jurisprudence, which was upwards of one hundred years old." Continuing, Mr. Wickham said: "What, sir, is the tendency of this application? What is the motion? I have no doubt, the gentlemen mean to act correctly—I wish to cast no imputation; but the counsel and the court well know that there are a set of busy people (not I hope employed by the Government) who, thinking to do right, are laboring to ruin the reputation of my client. I do not charge the Government with this attempt; but the thing is actually done. Attempts have been made. The press from one end of the continent to the other, has been enlisted on their side to excite prejudice against Colonel Burr. Prejudice? Yes, they have influenced the public opinion by such representations, and by persons not passing between the prisoner and his country, but by *ex parte* evidence and mutilated statements. Ought not this court to bar the door as much as possible, against such misrepresentation? to shut out every effort to excite further prejudice, until the case is decided by a sworn jury? Not by the floating rumors of the day, but by the evidence of sworn witnesses?"

In reply to Mr. Botts and Mr. Wickham, Mr. Wirt for the first time addressed the court:

"Where is the crime," said Mr. Wirt, "of considering Aaron Burr a subject to the ordinary operation of the human passions? Towards any other man, it seems, the attorney would have been justified in using precautions against alarms and escapes; it is only improper when applied to this man. Really, sir, I recollect nothing in the history of his deportment which renders it so very incredible, that Aaron Burr would fly from a prosecution. But at all events, the attorney is bound to act on general principles, and to take care that justice be had against every person accused, by whatever name he may be called, or by whatever previous reputation he may be distinguished. This motion, however, it seems, is not legal at this time, because there is a grand jury in session. The amount of the position is, that though it may be generally true, that the court possesses the power to hear and commit, yet, if there be a grand jury, the power of the court is suspended; and the commitment cannot be had unless in consequence of a presentment or bill of indictment found by that body. The general power of the court being admitted, those who rely on this exception, should support it by authority; and, therefore, the *loud call* for precedents, which we have heard from the other side come improperly from that quarter. We ground this motion in the general power of the court to commit: let those who say that this general power is destroyed by the presence of a grand jury show one precedent to countenance this original and extraordinary motion. I believe, sir, I may safely affirm, that not a single reported case or dictum can be found, which has the most distant bearing towards such an idea. Sir, no such dictum or case ought to exist. It would be unreasonable and destructive of the principles of justice.

"But, sir, we are told, that the investigation is calculated to keep alive the public prejudice; and we hear great complaints about these public prejudices. The country is represented as being filled with misrepresentations and calumnies against Aaron Burr; the public indignation, it is said, is already sufficiently excited. This argument is also inapplicable to our right to make this motion; it does not affect the legality of our procedure. Sir, if Aaron Burr be innocent instead of resisting this motion, he ought to hail it with triumph and exultation. What is it that we propose to introduce? Not the rumors that are floating through the world, nor the *bulk* of the multitude, nor the speculations of newspapers, but the *evidence of facts*. We propose, that the whole evidence exculpatory as well as accusative, shall come before you; instead of exciting, this is the true mode of correcting, prejudices. The world, which it is said has been misled and influenced by falsehood, will now hear the truth. Let the truth come out, let us know how much of what we have heard is false, how much of it is true; how much of what we feel is prejudice, how much of it is justified by fact. Whoever before heard of such an apprehension as that which is professed on the other side? *Prejudice excited by evidence!* Evidence, sir, is the great corrector of prejudice. Why then does Aaron Burr shrink from it? It is strange to me that a man, who complains so much of being, without cause, illegally seized and transported by a military officer, should be afraid to confront the evidence; evidence can be promotive only of truth. I repeat it then, sir, why does he shrink from the evidence? The gentlemen on the other side can give the answer. On our part we are ready to produce that evidence.

"The gentleman assures us, that no imputation is meant against the Government. Oh no, sir; Colonel Burr indeed has been oppressed, has been persecuted; but far be it from the gentleman to charge the Government with it. Colonel Burr indeed has been harassed by a military tyrant, who is 'the instrument of the Government bound to blind obedience'; but the gentleman could not by any means be understood as intending to insinuate aught to the prejudice of the Government. The gentleman is understood, sir; his object is correctly understood. He would divert the public attention from Aaron Burr and point it to another quarter. He would, too, if he could, shift the popular displeasure, which he has spoken of, from Aaron Burr to another quarter. These remarks were not intended for your ear, sir; they were intended for the people who surround us; they can have no effect upon the mind of the court. I am too well acquainted with the dignity, the firmness, the illumination of this bench, to apprehend any such consequence. But the gentlemen would balance the account of popular prejudices; they would convert the judicial inquiry into a political question; they would make it a question between Thomas Jefferson and Aaron Burr. The purpose is well understood, sir; but it shall not be served. I will not degrade the administration of this country by entering on their defence. Besides, sir, this is not our business; at present we have an account to settle, not between Aaron Burr and Thomas Jefferson, but between Aaron Burr and the laws of his country. Let us finish his trial first. The administration, too, will be tried before their country; before the world. They, sir, I believe, will never shrink, either from the evidence or the verdict."

Mr. Hay then delivered an elaborate argument in support of his motion and was followed by Mr. Randolph. Colonel Burr concluded the debate in a ten minutes' speech.

"The case is this," says Colonel Burr: "No man denies the authority of the court, to commit for a crime; but no commitment ought to be made, except on probable cause. This authority is necessary; because policy requires, that there should be some power to bind an accused individual for his personal appearance, until there shall have been sufficient time to obtain witnesses for his trial; but this power ought to be controlled as much as possible.

"The question in the present case, is whether there is probable cause of guilt; and whether time ought to be allowed to collect testimony against me. This time ought generally to be limited;

but there is no precise standard on the subject; and much is of course left to the sound discretion of the court. Two months ago, however, you declared that there had been time enough to collect the evidence necessary to commit, on probable cause; and surely, if this argument was good then, it is still better now.

"As soon as a prosecutor has notice of a crime, he generally looks out for witnesses. It is his object to obtain probable cause for committing the accused. Five months ago, a high authority declared that there was a crime; that I was at the head of it; and it mentioned the very place, too, where the crime was in a state of preparation. The principal witness against me, is said to be Mr. Wilkinson. Now, from what period is the time to be computed? If, from the time I was suspected, five months; if, from the time when I was seized, three months; or is it to be only computed from the time when I was committed? So that it is near forty days since the notice must have arrived at New Orleans. But a vessel navigates the coast, from New Orleans to Norfolk, in three weeks. I contend, however, that witnesses ought to be produced, from the very time when the crimes are said to be committed. There is, then, no apology for the delay of the prosecution, as far as it respects the only person for whom an apology is attempted to be made.

"There are other serious objections to my situation. Must I be ready to proceed to trial? True, sir, but then it must be in their own way. Are we then on equal terms here? Certainly not. And again, as to affidavits. The United States can have compulsory process to obtain them; but I have no such advantage. An *ex parte* evidence, then, is brought before this court, on a motion for commitment. The evidence on one side only is exhibited; but if I had mine also to adduce, it would probably contradict and counteract the evidence for the United States. Well, sir, and these affidavits are put into the newspapers, and they fall into the hands of the grand jury. I have no such means as these, sir; and where then is the equality between the Government and myself.

"The opinion of the court, too, is to be committed against me. Is this no evil?

"A sufficient answer, sir, has been given to the argument about my delay; and its disadvantages to myself have been ably developed. But my counsel have been charged with declamation against the Government of the United States. I certainly, sir, shall not be charged with declamation; but surely it is an established principle, sir, that no government is so high as to be beyond the reach of criticism; and it is more particularly laid down, that this vigilance is more peculiarly necessary, when any government institutes a prosecution: and one reason is, on account of the vast disproportion of means which exists between it and the accused. But, if ever there was a case which justified this vigilance, it is certainly the present one, when the Government has displayed such uncommon activity. If, then, this Government has been so peculiarly active against me, it is not improper to make the assertion here, for the purpose of increasing the circumspection of the court."

Mr. Burr observed, that he meant by persecution, the harassing of any individual, contrary to the forms of law; and that his case, unfortunately, presented too many instances of this description. He would merely state a few of them. He said that his friends had been everywhere seized by the military authority; a practice truly consonant with European despotisms. He said that persons had been dragged by compulsory process before particular tribunals, and compelled to give testimony against him. His papers, too, had been seized. "And yet, in England," said he, "where we say they know nothing of liberty, a gentleman, who had been seized and detained two hours, in a back parlour, had obtained damages to the amount of one thousand guineas." He said that an order had been issued to kill him, as he was descending the Mississippi, and seize his property. And yet, they could only have killed his person, even if he had been formally condemned for treason. He said that even post-offices had been broken open, and robbed of his papers; that, in the Mississippi Territory, even an indictment was about to be laid against the postmaster; that he had always taken this for a felony; but that nothing seemed too extravagant to be forgiven by the amiable morality of this Government. "All this," said Mr. Burr, "may only prove that my case is a solitary exception from the general rule. The Government may be tender, mild and humane to everybody but me. If so, to be sure it is of little consequence to anybody but myself. But surely I may be excused if I complain a little of such proceedings."

AFFIDAVIT OF BURR FOR SUBPŒNA *DUCES TECUM* FOR PRESIDENT JEFFERSON

"Our President," said Mr. Burr, "is a lawyer and a great one too. He certainly ought to know what it is that constitutes a war. Six months ago, he proclaimed that there was a civil war. And yet, for six months have they been hunting for it, and still cannot find one spot where it existed. There was, to be sure, a most terrible war in the newspapers; but nowhere else."

The next day the court in a written opinion held that the motion was a proper one at this stage of the proceedings, and the attorney for the United States was permitted to open his testimony; but in doing so, the Chief Justice expressed his regrets that the result of the motion "may be publications unfavorable to the justice and to the right decision of the case." Counsel were impressed with this observation of the court, and an attempt was made to reach an agreement whereby a public disclosure of the evidence at this time might be avoided. It was proposed by counsel for the United States that Colonel Burr's recognizance be made sufficiently large to insure his appearance to answer the charge of high treason against the United States, but on the following day this proposition was rejected by Colonel Burr. Mr. Hay then proceeded with some

- 17 -

reluctance to the examination of witnesses in support of his motion to commit Burr, as "he felt the full force of the objections to a disclosure of the evidence, and the necessity of the court declaring its opinion before the case was laid before the jury."

The attorney for the United States first sought to read the deposition of General Wilkinson, which precipitated the question of the order in which the testimony was to be introduced and its admissibility. The Supreme Court had already decided in the case of Swartout and Bollman that the deposition of Wilkinson might be admitted in evidence under certain circumstances, but that it did not contain any proof of an overt act. The Chief Justice observed that no evidence certainly had any bearing upon the present case unless the overt act be proved, but he would permit the attorney for the United States to pursue his own course as to the order of introducing his testimony.

A lengthy argument here ensued, in which Mr. Botts took a conspicuous part. In a most lucid manner he defined the crime of high treason under the Constitution of the United States, and applied it to the issue before the court.

"First," he said, "it must be proved that there was an actual war. A war consists wholly in acts, and not in intentions. The acts must be in themselves acts of war; and if they be not so intrinsically, words or intentions cannot make them so. In England, when conspiring the death of the King was treason, the *quo animo* formed the essence of the offence; but, in America, the national convention has confined treason to the act. We cannot have a constructive war within the meaning of the Constitution. An intention to levy war, is not evidence that a war was levied. Intentions are always mutable and variable; the continuance of guilty intentions is not to be presumed. Secondly, the war must not only have been levied, but Colonel Burr must be proved to have committed an overt act of treason in that war. A treasonable intention to coöperate is no evidence of an actual coöperation. The acts of others, even if in pursuance of his plan, would be no evidence against him. It might not be necessary that he should be present, perhaps; but he must be, at the time of levying the war, coöperating by acts, or, in the language of the Constitution, be committing overt acts. Thirdly, the overt act by the accused, as an actual war, must not only be proved, but it must be proved to have been committed within this district. Fourthly, the overt act must be proved by two witnesses."

The Chief Justice declared this view of the law to be correct, and General Wilkinson's deposition was accordingly put aside.

Mr. Hay realized the utter futility of his efforts to commit Burr on the charge of treason at this stage of the case, and readily consented to Burr's proposition to double the amount of his bond to answer the charge of a misdemeanor. Luther Martin, who appeared for the first time, became one of his sureties. He declared in open court that he was happy to have this opportunity to give a public proof of his confidence in the honor of Colonel Burr, and of his belief in his innocence.

General Wilkinson had not as yet put in his appearance, and much impatience was manifested because of the inconvenience he had caused. The grand jury were therefore adjourned from day to day until the second day of June, when they were adjourned until the 9th, on which last named day he was expected to arrive.

The court met accordingly on the 9th, and after the names of the grand jury had been called and explanations offered as to the continued absence of General Wilkinson, Colonel Burr moved the court to issue a subpœna *duces tecum* addressed to the President of the United States, requiring him to produce certain papers, and on the following day he presented to the court an affidavit, drawn up and sworn to by himself in open court in support of his motion. In this affidavit he sets forth that he has great reason to believe, that a letter from General Wilkinson to the President of the United States, dated October 21st, 1806, as mentioned in the President's message of the 22nd January, 1807, to both Houses of Congress, together with the documents accompanying the said letter, and copy of the answer of said Thomas Jefferson, or of anyone by his authority, to the said letter, may be material in his defence in the prosecution against him. And further that he has reason to believe, the military and naval orders given by the president of the United States, through the departments of war and of the navy, to the officers of the army and navy, at or near New Orleans stations, touching or concerning the said Burr, or his property, will also be material in his defense; and that he had made a personal request for copies of these papers during a recent visit to Washington, and had been refused.

Mr. Martin in support of the propriety of granting this particular subpœna laid down as a general principle, in all civil or criminal cases, that every man had a right by process to establish his rights or his innocence. He asserted that one of the papers necessary to the defense is the original letter from General Wilkinson described in Burr's affidavit. The other papers are copies of official orders by the navy and war departments. He had supposed that every citizen was entitled to such copies of official papers as are material to him, and he had never heard of but one instance where they were refused, and this was under presidential influence.

"We intend to show," says Mr. Martin, "that, by this particular order, his property and his person were to be destroyed; yes, by these tyrannical orders, the life and property of an innocent man were to be exposed to destruction. We did not expect these originals themselves. But we did apply for copies; and were refused under presidential influence. In New York, in the farcical trials of Ogden and Smith, the officers of the Government screened themselves from attending, under the sanction of the President's name. Perhaps the same farce may be repeated here; and it is for this reason that we applied directly to the President of the United States. Whether it would have been best to have applied to the Secretaries of State, of the Navy and War, I cannot say. All that we want is the copies of some papers, and the original of another. This is a peculiar case, sir. The President has undertaken to prejudge this trial by declaring, that, 'of his guilt there can be no doubt.' He has assumed to himself the knowledge of the Supreme Being himself, and pretended to search the heart of my highly respected friend. He has proclaimed him a traitor in the face of that country, which has rewarded him. He has let slip the dogs of war, the hell-hounds of persecution, to hunt down my friend. And would this President of the United States, who has raised all of this absurd clamor, pretend to keep back the papers which are wanted for this trial, where life is at stake? It is a sacred principle, that in all such cases, the accused has a right to all the evidence which is necessary to his defense. And whoever withholds, wilfully, information that would save the life of a person, charged with a capital offence, is substantially a murderer, and so recorded in the registry of Heaven."

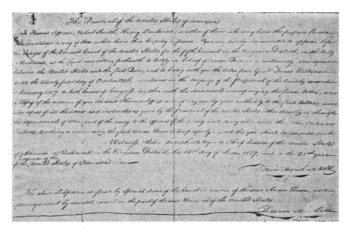

SUBPŒNA *DUCES TECUM* FOR PRESIDENT
JEFFERSON

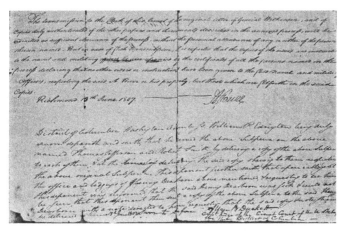

SUBPŒNA *DUCES TECUM* FOR PRESIDENT
JEFFERSON (Continued)

Mr. Wirt replied to Mr. Martin, and in the course of his argument, made the following reference to Martin's arraignment of Jefferson and the administration:

"I cannot take my seat, sir, without expressing my deep and sincere sorrow at the policy which the gentlemen in the defense have thought it necessary to adopt. As to Mr. Martin, I should have been willing to impute this fervid language to the sympathies and resentments of that friendship which he has taken such frequent occasions to express for the prisoner, his honourable friend. In the cause of friendship I can pardon zeal even up to the point of intemperance; but the truth is, sir, that before Mr. Martin came to Richmond, this policy was settled, and on every question incidentally brought before the court, we were stunned with invectives against the administration. I appeal to your recollection, sir, whether this policy was not manifested even so early as in those new and until now unheard of challenges to the grand jury for favour? Whether that policy was not followed up with increased spirit, in the very first speeches which were made in this case; those of Mr. Botts and Mr. Wickham on their previous question pending the attorney's motion to commit? Whether they have not seized with avidity every subsequent occasion, and on every mere question of abstract law before the court, flew off at a tangent from the subject, to launch into declamations against the government? Exhibiting the prisoner continually as a persecuted patriot; a Russell or a Sidney, bleeding under the scourge of a despot, and dying for virtue's sake! If there be any truth in the charges against him, how different were the purposes of his soul from those of a Russell or a Sidney! I beg to know what gentlemen can intend, expect, or hope, from these perpetual philippics against the Government? Do they flatter themselves that this court feel political prejudices which will supply the place of argument and innocence on the part of the prisoner? Their conduct amounts to an insinuation of the sort. But I do not believe it. On the contrary, I feel the firm and pleasing assurance, that as to the court, the beam of their judgment will remain steady, although the earth itself should shake under the concussion of prejudice. Or is it on the bystanders that the gentlemen expect to make a favourable impression? And do they use the court merely as a canal, through which they may pour upon the world their undeserved invectives against the Government? Do they wish to divide the popular resentment and diminish thereby their own quota? Before the gentlemen arraign the administration, let them clear the skirts of their client. Let them prove his innocence; let them prove that he has not covered himself with the clouds of mystery and just suspicion; let them prove that he has been all along erect and fair, in open day, and that these charges against him are totally groundless and false. That will be the most eloquent invective which they can pronounce against the prosecution; but until they prove this innocence, it shall be in vain that they attempt to divert our minds to other objects, and other inquiries. We will keep our eyes on Aaron Burr until he satisfies our utmost scruple. I beg to know, sir, if the course which gentlemen pursue is not disrespectful to the court itself? Suppose there are any foreigners here accustomed to regular government in their own country, what can they infer from hearing the federal administration thus reviled to the federal judiciary? Hearing the judiciary told, that the administration are 'Bloodhounds, hunting this man with a keen and savage thirst for blood; that they now suppose they have hunted him into their toils and have him safe.' Sir, no man, foreigner or citizen, who hears this language addressed to the court, and received with all the complacency at least which silence can imply, can make any inferences from it very honourable to the court. It would only be inferred, while they are thus suffered to roll and luxuriate in these gross invectives against the administration, that they are furnishing the joys of a Mahometan paradise to the court as well as to their client. I hope that the court, for their own sakes, will compel a decent respect to that government of which they themselves form a branch. On our part, we wish only a fair trial of this case. If the man be innocent, in the name of God let him go; but while we are on the question of his guilt or innocence, let us not suffer our attention and judgment to be diverted and distracted by the introduction of other subjects foreign to the inquiry."

The counsel for the prosecution admitted that the President of the United States was amenable to an ordinary subpœna *ad testificandum* as any other citizen, but that the application for a subpœna *duces tecum* was addressed to the discretion of the court, and did not issue as a process of right. Besides, the papers required to be produced by such a process must be shown to be material for the defense. They questioned the propriety of compelling the chief magistrate to produce in court any papers in his possession not public in its character. They further contended that until the grand jury had found a true bill and the prosecutor had announced his intention to proceed to a trial thereon the prisoner had no right to legal process.

After five days of debate the Chief Justice delivered an elaborate opinion on the motion of Colonel Burr. He decided that the subpœna *duces tecum* directed to the president of the United States might issue. He held that any person charged with a crime in the courts of the United States has a right, before, as well as after indictment, to the process of the court to compel the attendance of his witnesses; that in the provisions of the Constitution, and of the statutes which give to the accused a right to the compulsory process of the court, there is no exception whatever.

"If, upon any principle," said the Chief Justice, "the President could be construed to stand exempt from the general provisions of the Constitution, it would be because his duties, as chief magistrate, demand his whole time for national objects. But it is apparent that this demand is not unremitting; and, if it should exist at the time when his attendance on a court, is required, it would be sworn on the return of the subpœna, and would rather constitute a reason for not obeying the process of the court, than a reason against it being issued. The guard furnished to this high office to protect him from being harassed by vexatious and unnecessary subpœnas, is to be looked for in the conduct of a court after those subpœnas have issued; not in any circumstance which is to precede their being issued. If, in being summoned to give his personal attendance to testify, the law does not discriminate between the President and a private citizen, what foundation is there for the opinion, that this difference is created by the circumstance, that his testimony depends on a paper in his possession, not on facts, which come to his knowledge otherwise than by writing? The court can perceive no foundation for such an opinion. The propriety of introducing any paper into a case, as testimony, must depend on the character of the paper, not on the character of the person who holds it. A subpœna *duces tecum*, then, may issue to any person to whom any ordinary subpœna may issue, directing him to bring any paper of which the party praying it has a right to avail himself as testimony; if, indeed, that be the necessary process for obtaining the view of such paper."

The decision of the Chief Justice and the strictures of Martin threw Jefferson into a violent rage. We find him promptly writing to Mr. Hay, "Shall we move to commit Luther Martin as *particeps criminis* with Burr? Grayball will fix upon him misprision of treason at least, and, at any rate, his evidence will pull down this unprincipled and impudent Federal bull-dog, and add another proof that the most clamorous defenders of Burr are all his accomplices." And again he writes to Hay, after discussing at length the intimation in the decision of the Chief Justice that even the bodily presence of the President might be compelled by the court, which proposition he indignantly denied, "that the leading feature of our Constitution is the independence of the legislative, executive and judiciary of each other; and none are more jealous of this than the judiciary. But would the executive be independent of the judiciary if he were subject to the commands of the latter, and to imprisonment for disobedience, if the smaller courts could bandy him from pillar to post, keep him constantly trudging from North to South and East and West and withdraw him entirely from his executive duties?"

The law and reasoning of the decision of the Chief Justice were convincing. Jefferson knew that under the Constitution the President had no superior right to those of any other citizen, and, while directing substantially all papers required by the subpœna *duces tecum* to be furnished, he refused to appear in person in court. He openly defied the process of the court. He intimated that if the court attempted to enforce its writ he would meet force with force. The Chief Justice realized what this meant, and the matter was quietly dropped.

On Saturday, June 13th, twenty-two days after the court had convened, General Wilkinson arrived in the city of Richmond, and on the following Monday he was sworn and sent to the grand jury, with a notification that it would facilitate their inquiries if they would examine him immediately.

Wilkinson was at the head of the army and Governor of the territory of Louisiana, to which latter office he had been appointed about the close of the session of Congress that Burr as Vice-President presided over the Senate. Between him and Burr a long friendship had existed. They had been fellow soldiers in the War of the Revolution—had shared together the hardships of the winter of 1775–6, and the perils of the unsuccessful attack on the city of Quebec. While it was true they had seen very little of each other since the war they had at intervals, and only a short time before the arrest of Burr, corresponded confidentially and in cipher. He was undoubtedly in the secrets of Burr, until he saw the impending explosion, and then he became active in exposing the plot and bringing Burr to trial. Certain it is that Burr regarded him as an associate and denounced his treachery.

The meeting between Burr and his former friend Wilkinson was dramatic, and is graphically described by Washington Irving.

"Burr," says Irving, "was seated with his back to the entrance, facing the judges, and conversing with one of his counsel when Wilkinson strutted into the court and took a stand in a parallel line with Burr on his right hand. Here he stood for a moment swelling like a turkey cock, and bracing himself up for the encounter of Burr's eyes. The latter did not take any notice of him until the Judge directed the clerk to swear General Wilkinson; at the mention of the name Burr turned his head, looked him full in the face with one of his piercing regards, swept his eye over his whole person from head to foot, as if to scan its dimensions and then cooly resumed his former position, and went on conversing with his counsel as tranquilly as ever. The whole look was over in an instant, but it was an admirable one. There was no appearance of study or constraint in it; no affectation of disdain or defiance; a slight expression of contempt played over his countenance, such as you would show on regarding any person to whom you were indifferent, but whom you considered mean and contemptible."

The examination of witnesses by the grand jury continued from day to day until June 24th, when in the midst of an argument by Mr. Botts for an attachment against General Wilkinson for endeavoring to prevent the free course of testimony, the grand jury entered the courtroom, and speaking through its distinguished foreman, stated that they had agreed upon several indictments, which he handed to the clerk of the court. The clerk then read the following endorsements thereon:

"An indictment against Aaron Burr for treason—a true bill."

"An indictment against Aaron Burr for a misdemeanor—a true bill."

"An indictment against Herman Blannerhassett for treason— a true bill."

"An indictment against Herman Blannerhassett for a misdemeanor—a true bill."

The grand jury then adjourned until the next day, and at the conclusion of Mr. Bott's argument on the motion for attachment, Colonel Burr with his wonted serene and placid air arose and stated to the court, that as true bills had been found against him, it was probable, the United States Attorney would move for his commitment; he would, however, suggest two ideas for the consideration of the court. "One was that it was within their discretion to bail in certain cases, even when the punishment was death; and the other was, that it was expedient for the court to exercise their discretion in this instance, as he should prove, that the indictment against him had been obtained by perjury."

Mr. Hay moved for his commitment. He stated that if the court had the power to bail, it was only to be exercised according to their sound discretion. After much time had been spent in debate, the Chief Justice observed that "he was under the necessity of committing Colonel Burr." He was accordingly committed to the custody of the Marshal, and conducted to the city jail, for the County of Henrico and the City of Richmond; but two days later on the affidavit of his counsel, who had visited him in his confinement, that the miserable state of the prison would endanger his health, and that it was so arranged as to deprive him of consultation with his counsel, and upon the further report of the Surveyor of the Public Buildings of the United States, the court entered the following order:

"Whereupon, it is ordered, that the Marshal of this district, do cause the front room of the house now occupied by Luther Martin, Esq., which room has been and is used as a dining room, to be prepared for the reception and safe-keeping of Colonel Aaron Burr, by securing the shutters to the windows of the said room by bars, and the door by a strong bar or pad-lock. And that he employ a guard of seven men to be placed on the floor of the adjoining unfinished house, and on the same story with the before described front room, and also, at the door opening into the said front room; and upon the Marshal's reporting to the court that the said room has been so fitted up, and the guard employed, that then the said Marshal be directed, and he is hereby directed, to remove to the said room, the body of the said Aaron Burr from the public gaol, there to be by him safely kept."

This building now known as Blair's Drug Store, still stands at the corner of Ninth and Broad Streets, in the City of Richmond, Virginia.

The grand jury had on the day previous brought in indictments for treason against Ex-Senator Jonathan Dayton of New Jersey, Ex-Senator John Smith of Ohio, Comfort Tyler and Israel Smith of New York; and Davis Floyd of the territory of Indiana. This completed their inquiries, and after an appropriate address by the Chief Justice in which he complimented them upon the great patience and cheerful attention with which they had performed the arduous and laborious duties in which they had been so long engaged, discharged them from further attendance on the court.

After some discussion as to procedure, the clerk of the court read the indictment against Burr, for treason against the United States, which with the endorsements thereon (exclusive of the verdict of the trial jury), is as follows:

"VIRGINIA DISTRICT:

"IN THE CIRCUIT COURT OF THE UNITED STATES OF AMERICA, IN AND FOR THE FIFTH CIRCUIT AND VIRGINIA DISTRICT:

"The grand inquest of the United States of America, for the Virginia district, upon their oath do present that Aaron Burr, late of the city of New York, and State of New York, Attorney at Law, being an inhabitant of and residing within the United States, and under the protection of the laws of the United States, and owing allegiance and fidelity to the same United States, not having the fear of God before his eyes, nor weighing the duty of his said allegiance, but being moved and seduced by the instigation of the devil, wickedly devising and intending the peace and tranquillity of the said United States to disturb and to stir, move and excite insurrection, rebellion and war against the said United States, on the tenth day of December in the year of Christ one thousand eight hundred and six at a certain place called and known by the name of Blannerhassett's Island, in the county of Wood and District of Virginia aforesaid, and within the jurisdiction of this Court, with force and arms unlawfully, falsely, maliciously and traitorously did compass, imagine and intend to raise and levy war, insurrection and rebellion against the said United States; and in order to fulfil and bring to effect the said traitorous compassings, imaginations and intentions of him, the said Aaron Burr, he, the said Aaron Burr, afterwards, to wit, on the said tenth day of December in the year one thousand eight hundred and six aforesaid, at the said island, called Blannerhassett's Island as aforesaid, in the County of Wood aforesaid in the District of Virginia aforesaid and within the jurisdiction of this Court, with a great multitude of persons whose names at present are unknown to the grand inquest aforesaid, to a great number, to wit, to the number of thirty persons and upwards, armed and arrayed in a warlike manner, that is to say, with guns, swords, and dirks and other warlike weapons as well offensive as defensive, being then and there unlawfully, maliciously and traitorously assembled and gathered together, did falsely and traitorously assemble and join themselves together against the said United States, and then and there with force and arms did falsely and traitorously, and in warlike and hostile manner, array and dispose themselves against the said United States, and then and there that is to say on the day and in the year aforesaid at the island aforesaid commonly called Blannerhassett's Island in the County aforesaid of Wood, within the Virginia district, and the jurisdiction of this Court, in pursuance of such their traitorous intentions and purposes, aforesaid, he the said Aaron Burr with the said persons so as aforesaid traitorously assembled and armed and arrayed in manner aforesaid, most wickedly, maliciously and traitorously did ordain, prepare and levy war against the said United States, contrary to the duty of their said allegiance and fidelity, against the Constitution, peace and dignity of the said United States, and against the form of the Act of Congress of the said United States, in such case made and provided:

"And the grand inquest of the United States of America for the Virginia district upon their oaths aforesaid do further present, that the said Aaron Burr, late of the City of New York, and State of New York, attorney at law, being an inhabitant of and residing within the United States and under the protection of the laws of the United States, and owing allegiance and fidelity to the same United States, not having the fear of God before his eyes, nor weighing the duty of his said allegiance, but being moved and seduced by the instigation of the devil, wickedly devising and intending the peace and tranquillity of the United States to disturb, and to stir, move, and excite insurrection, rebellion and war against the said United States, on the eleventh day of December in the year of our Lord one thousand eight hundred and six, at a certain place, called and known by the name of Blannerhassett's Island in the County of Wood and District of Virginia aforesaid and within the jurisdiction of this court, with force and arms, unlawfully, falsely, maliciously and traitorously did compass, imagine and intend to raise and levy war, insurrection and rebellion against the said United States, and in order to fulfil and bring to effect the said traitorous compassings, imaginations and intentions of him the said Aaron Burr, he, the said Aaron Burr, afterwards, to wit, on the said last mentioned day of December in the year one thousand eight hundred and six aforesaid, at a certain place commonly called and known by the name of Blannerhassett's Island in the said County of Wood, in the District of Virginia aforesaid, and within the jurisdiction of this court, with one other great multitude of persons, whose names at present are unknown to the grand inquest aforesaid, to a great number, to wit, to the number of thirty persons and upwards, armed and arrayed in a warlike manner, that is to say, with guns, swords and dirks, and other warlike weapons as well offensive as defensive being then and there unlawfully, maliciously and traitorously assembled and gathered together, did falsely and traitorously assemble and join themselves together against the said United States, and then and there with force and arms did falsely and traitorously and in a warlike and hostile manner, array and dispose themselves against the said United States, and then and there, that is to say, on the day and in the year last mentioned, at the island aforesaid in the County of Wood aforesaid, in the Virginia district, and within the jurisdiction of this Court, in pursuance of such their traitorous intentions, and purposes aforesaid, he the said Aaron Burr with the said persons so as aforesaid traitorously assembled and armed and arrayed in manner aforesaid, most wickedly, maliciously and traitorously did ordain, prepare and levy war against the said United States, and further to fulfil and carry into effect the said traitorous compassings, imaginations and intentions of the said Aaron Burr against the said United States, and to carry on the war thus levied as aforesaid against the said United States, the said Aaron Burr with the multitude last mentioned at the island aforesaid, in the said County of Wood, within the Virginia district aforesaid and within the jurisdiction of this, did array themselves in a warlike manner, with guns and other weapons offensive and defensive, and did proceed from the said island down the river Ohio, in the County aforesaid within the Virginia district, and within the jurisdiction of this Court, on the said eleventh day of December in the year one thousand eight hundred and six aforesaid, with the wicked and traitorous intention to descend the said river and the river Mississippi and by force and arms traitorously to take possession of a City commonly called New Orleans in the territory of Orleans belonging to the United States; contrary to the duty of their said allegiance and fidelity, against the Constitution, peace and dignity of the said United States and against the form of the Act of the Congress of the United States in such case made and provided.

HAY.

Attorney of the United States for the Virginia District.

"Witness in behalf of the United States.

1. Thomas Truxton
2. Stephen Decatur
3. Benjamin Stoddert
4. William Eaton
5. William Duane
6. Erick Bollman
7. Peter Taylor
8. Jacob Allbright
9. Charles Willie
10. John Graham
11. Saml. Swartout
12. Julien Dupeistre
13. Prevost
14. James Miller
15. Saml. Kouten
16. George Morgan
17. John Morgan
18. Thomas Morgan
19. Nicholas Perkins
20. Robert Spence
21. George Harris
22. Cyrus Jones
23. Thomas Peterkin
24. Elias Glover
25. Simeon Poole
26. Dudley Woodbridge
27. David C. Wallace
28. Edward W. Tupper

29. Edmund B. Dana
30. James Read
31. John G. Henderson
32. Alex. Henderson
34. Ambrose Smith
35. Hugh Phelps
36. Gen. Wilkinson
37. Dunbaugh
38. Charles Lindsay
39. John Manhatton
40. James Knox
41. William Love
42. David Fisk
43. Thomas Heartly
44. Stephen S. Welch
45. James Kenney
46. Samuel Moxley
47. Edw. P. Gaines
48. A. D. Smith."

ENDORSED:

"United States
vs.
Aaron Burr.
Indictment for Treason.

A true Bill.
John Randolph."

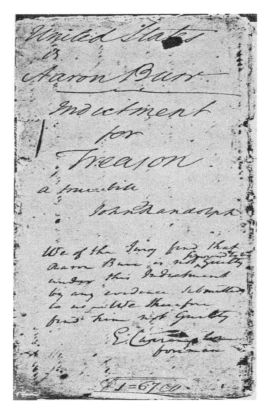

FINDINGS OF THE GRAND AND PETIT JURIES

At the conclusion of the reading of the indictment, Mr. Burr addressed the court as follows:

"I acknowledge myself to be the person named in the indictment: I plead *not guilty*; and put myself upon my country for trial."

The indictment, as will be observed, specifies the place of the overt act to be at Blannerhassett Island, and the time the 10th day of December, 1806.

The court, when the plea was in, made an order for a venire of forty-eight jurors, twelve of whom, at least, were to be summoned from Wood County and on the following day, June 27th, the court ordered the *venire facias* to issue to the marshal, returnable on the 3rd day of August and fixed that day for the trial.

Three days later Burr was, on motion of the United States attorney, removed from his lodging at the corner of Ninth and Broad Streets, and, with the approval of the Governor of Virginia, placed in the third story of the penitentiary, therein to be confined, until the 2nd day of August.

The court pursuant to adjournment met promptly at 12 o'clock, Monday, August 3rd, in the House of Delegates, with Chief Justice Marshal presiding. Judge Griffin, the District Judge, who had heretofore set in the case, did not appear until the following Friday.

George Hay, William Wirt and Alexander MacRae appeared as counsel for the prosecution, and Edmund Randolph, John Wickham, Benjamin Botts, John Baker and Luther Martin for the prisoner. Mr. Charles Lee appeared about two weeks later.

The court room was crowded with an immense throng of citizens, when Burr, accompanied by his son-in-law, Governor Alston, of South Carolina, and exhibiting his usual serenity and self-possession, entered. The names of the jurors were promptly called, and shortly thereafter the court adjourned until the following Wednesday, to give counsel for the defense time to examine the list of the jurors summoned.

The court met pursuant to adjournment, and for twelve days was engaged in the selection of a jury for the trial of the case. Of the original venire of forty-eight, only four, Richard E. Parker, David Lambert, Hugh Mercer, and Edward Carrington were elected, and, of the second venire for a like number, eight were accepted as competent jurors, namely, Christopher Anthony, James Sheppard, Reuben Blakey, Miles Bottes, Henry C. Coleman, Benjamin Graves, John M. Sheppard, and Richard Curd.

The jury now being elected and sworn, the prisoner was directed to stand up. The clerk read the indictment for treason against him, and, at the conclusion of the reading, addressed the jury in the usual form. The case was then opened for the prosecution by Mr. Hay, it being agreed that he should fully present the side of the government, and immediately thereafter proceed with his evidence.

Mr. Hay dwelt at great length on the crime of treason.

"In Great Britain," he said, "there are no less than ten different species of treason; at least that was the number when Blakstone wrote, and it is possible that the number may have been increased since. But in this country, where the principle is established in the Constitution, there are only two descriptions of treason; and the number being fixed in the Constitution itself, can never be increased by the legislature, however important and necessary it should be, in their opinion, that the number should be augmented. By the third section, article 3 of the Constitution of the United States, 'treason against the United States shall consist only in levying war against them, or in adhering to their enemies; giving them aid and comfort.' With respect to the latter description, there is no occasion to say anything, as the offense charged in the indictment is 'levying war against the United States'; but it adds that *'no person shall be convicted of treason, unless on the testimony of two witnesses to the same overt act, or on confession in open court.'"*

The first witness called was General Eaton. Colonel Burr objected to the order of the testimony. He said Mr. Hay had not stated the nature of the witness' testimony; but he presumed that it related to certain conversations said to have happened at Washington. He contended that no such evidence as that, which tended only to show intentions or designs, was admissible until an *overt* act of treason had been proved. This question was ably argued by counsel on both sides.

The next day the Chief Justice decided that so far as the testimony of General Eaton "relates to the fact charged in the indictment, so far as it relates to levying war on Blannerhassett's Island, so far as it relates to a design to seize on New Orleans, or to separate by force, the Western from the Atlantic states, it is deemed relevant and is now admissible: so far as it respects other plans to be executed in the City of Washington, or elsewhere, if it indicate a treasonable design, it is a design to commit a distinct act of treason, and is therefore not relevant to the present indictment. It can only, by showing a general evil intention, render it more probable that the intention in the particular case was evil. It is merely additional or corroborative testimony, and therefore, if admissible at any time, it is only admissible according to the rules and principles which the court must respect, after hearing that which it is to confirm."

General Eaton was then called to the stand and examined. He stated in the beginning that he knew nothing of any overt act of treason on the part of Burr, or of any of the happenings on

Blannerhassett's Island; but that he knew much concerning Burr's expressions of treasonable intentions.

The next witnesses called to prove treasonable designs were Commodore Truxton, Peter Taylor, Blannerhassett's gardener, and Colonel Morgan and his two sons.

The prosecution now took up the testimony to establish the *overt* act and called to the stand Jacob Allbright, Peter Taylor, William Love, Maurice P. Belknap and Edmund B. Dana. These witnesses proved the assemblage of men, some thirty or more, on Blannerhassett's Island, December 10th, 1806, armed with rifles and pistols, the pretended purpose of which was to descend the Ohio River to the City of New Orleans, and make it the base of operations in an expedition to Mexico; but failed to prove the act of levying war.

It was not proved that Burr was present on the Island when the assemblage of the men took place.

The only witness, who gave any direct testimony on the overt act sought to be proved was Allbright, and he was discredited on cross-examination. He testified on the night of the flight from the Island that "a man by the name of Tupper (meaning General Tupper), laid his hands upon Blannerhassett, and said: 'Your body is in my hands, in the name of the Commonwealth.' Some such words as that he mentioned. When Tupper made that motion, there were seven or eight muskets leveled at him. Tupper looked about him and said 'Gentlemen, I hope you will not do the like.' One of the gentlemen who was nearest about two yards off said 'I'd as leave as not.' Tupper then changed his speech, and said he wished him to escape safe down the river, and wished him luck."

At the conclusion of the evidence relating directly to the overt act charged in the indictment, counsel for the prosecution attempted to introduce collateral testimony of acts beyond the limits of the jurisdiction of the court; but Colonel Burr and his counsel strenuously objected to such testimony as wholly irrelevant and inadmissible, and moved the court to arrest the evidence on the ground that the United States had failed to prove an overt act, constituting treason, under the Constitution of the United States.

The argument on this motion, which was so vital to the further prosecution of the case commenced on the 20th of August, and continued until the 29th of that month, and was "doubtless," says Parton, "the finest display of legal knowledge and ability of which the history of the American bar can boast."

Mr. Wickham opened the debate and was followed by Randolph, Wirt, Botts, MacRae, Hay and Lee. Mr. Martin concluded. It fills one volume of Mr. Robertson's report of the case, and it would be vain to attempt in this brief review to give anything like a satisfactory account of it. Some of the reasons urged in support of the motion were: that Burr, not being present on Blannerhassett's Island, was merely an accessory, and not a principal; that if he was a principal he was a principal only in the second degree, where guilt is merely derivative, and that therefore no parole evidence could be admitted against him, until a record was produced of the conviction of the offenders in the first degree; that the facts must be proved as laid in the indictment, and evidence proving the accused to have been absent at the time of the overt acts is inadmissible to support an indictment charging him with the commission of that act; that no parole evidence could be given to connect the prisoner with the men assembled on Blannerhassett's Island, until an act of treason on the part of these men was proved; and that the assemblage there was not an act of treason; that until the fact of a crime is proved no evidence should be heard respecting the guilty intentions of the accused.

On Monday, August 31st the Chief Justice rendered his decision. He read it with great care and consumed three hours in doing so.

"The question now to be decided," he began, "has been argued in a manner worthy of its importance, and with an earnestness evincing the strong conviction felt by the counsel on each side that the law is with them.

"A degree of eloquence seldom displaced on any occasion has embellished a solidity of argument, and a depth of research by which the court has been greatly aided in forming the opinion it is about to deliver.

"The testimony adduced on the part of the United States to prove the overt act laid in the indictment having shown, and the attorney for the United States having admitted, that the prisoner was not present when that act, whatever may be its character, was committed, and there being no reason to doubt but that he was at a great distance and in a different state, it is objected to the testimony offered on the part of the United States, to connect him with those who committed the overt act, that such testimony is totally irrelevant and must therefore be rejected.

"The arguments in support of this motion respect in part the merits of the case as it may be supposed to stand independent of the pleadings, and in part as exhibited by the pleadings.

"On the first division of the subject two points are made:

"1st. That conformably to the constitution of the United States, no man can be convicted of treason who was not present when the war was levied.

"2d. That if this construction be erroneous, no testimony can be received to charge one man with the overt acts of others until those overt acts, as laid in the indictment, be proved to the satisfaction of the court.

"The question which arises on the construction of the constitution, in every point of view in which it can be contemplated, is of infinite moment to the people of this country and to their government, and requires the most temperate and the most deliberate consideration.

"Treason against the United States shall consist only in levying war against them."

The Chief Justice then proceeds to elaborately discuss an overt act of levying war. The opinion delivered by the Supreme Court in the case of Bollman and Swartout was declared by him to be not correctly understood; and that there must be, before an overt act of treason is completed, either the actual employment of force or a military assemblage of men, who are in a posture of war.

In conclusion the Chief Justice said:

"The law of the case being thus far settled; what ought to be the decision of the court on the present motion? Ought the court to sit and hear testimony which cannot affect the prisoner? or ought the court to arrest that testimony? On this question much has been said: much that may perhaps be ascribed to a misconception of the point really under consideration. The motion has been treated as a motion confessedly made to stop relevant testimony; and, in the course of the argument, it has been repeatedly stated, by those who oppose the motion, that irrelevant testimony may and ought to be stopped. That this statement is perfectly correct is one of those fundamental principles in judicial proceedings which is acknowledged by all, and is founded in the absolute necessity of the thing. No person will contend that, in a civil or criminal case, either party is at liberty to introduce what testimony he pleases, legal or illegal, and to consume the whole term in details of facts unconnected with the particular case. Some tribunal then must decide on the admissibility of testimony. The parties cannot constitute this tribunal; for they do not agree. The jury cannot constitute it; for the question is whether they shall hear the testimony or not. Who then but the court can constitute it? It is of necessity the peculiar province of the court to judge of the admissibility of testimony. If the court admit improper or reject proper testimony, it is an error of judgment; but it is an error committed in the direct exercise of their judicial functions.

"The present indictment charges the prisoner with levying war against the United States, and alleges an overt act of levying war. That overt act must be proved, according to the mandates of the constitution and of the act of congress, by two witnesses. It is not proved by a single witness. The presence of the accused has been stated to be an essential component part of the overt act in this indictment, unless the common law principle respecting accessories should render it unnecessary; and there is not only no witness who has proved his actual or legal presence, but the fact of his absence is not controverted. The counsel for the prosecution offer to give in evidence subsequent transactions at a different place and in a different state, in order to prove—what? the overt act laid in the indictment? that the prisoner was one of those who assembled at Blannerhassett's Island? No: that is not alleged. It is well known that such testimony is not competent to establish such a fact. The constitution and law require that the fact should be established by two witnesses; not by the establishment of other facts from which the jury might reason to this fact. The testimony then is not relevant. If it can be introduced, it is only in the character of corroboratives or confirmatory testimony, after the overt act has been proved by two witnesses in such manner that the question of fact ought to be left with the jury. The conclusion, that in this state of things no testimony can be admissible, is so inevitable that the counsel for the United States could not resist it. I do not understand them to deny, that, if the overt act be not proved by two witnesses so as to be submitted to the jury, all other testimony must be irrelevant; because no other testimony can prove the act. Now, an assemblage on Blannerhassett's Island is proved by the requisite number of witnesses; and the court might submit it to the jury whether that assemblage amounted to a levying of war; but the presence of the accused at that assemblage being nowhere alleged except in the indictment, the overt act is not proved by a single witness; and of consequence all other testimony must be irrelevant.

"The only difference between this motion as made, and the one in the form which the counsel for the United States would admit to be regular, is this: it is now general for the rejection of all testimony. It might be particular with respect to each witness as adduced. But can this be wished? or can it be deemed necessary? If enough be proved to show that the indictment cannot be supported, and that no testimony, unless it be of that description which the attorney for the United States declares himself not to possess, can be relevant, why should a question be taken on each witness?

"Much has been said in the course of the argument on points on which the court feels no inclination to comment particularly; but which may, perhaps, not improperly, receive some notice.

"That this court dares not usurp power is most true.

"That this court dares not shrink from its duty is not less true.

"No man is desirous of placing himself in a disagreeable situation. No man is desirous of becoming the peculiar subject of calumny. No man, might he let the bitter cup pass from him without self reproach, would drain it to the bottom. But if he have no choice in the case, if there be no alternative presented to him but a dereliction of duty or the opprobrium of those who are denominated the world, he merits the contempt as well as the indignation of his country who can hesitate which to embrace.

"That gentlemen, in a case the most interesting, in the zeal with which they advocate particular opinions, and under the conviction, in some measure produced by that zeal, should on each side press their arguments too far, should be impatient at any deliberation in the court, and should suspect or fear the operation of motives to which alone they can ascribe that deliberation, is perhaps a frailty incident to human nature; but if any conduct on the part of the court could warrant a sentiment that it would deviate to the one side or the other from the line prescribed by duty and by law, that conduct would be viewed by the judges themselves with an eye of extreme severity, and would long be recollected with deep and serious regret.

"The arguments on both sides have been intently and deliberately considered. Those which could not be noticed, since to notice every argument and authority would swell this opinion to a volume, have not been disregarded. The result of the whole is a conviction, as complete as the mind of the court is capable of receiving on a complex subject, that the motion must prevail.

"No testimony relative to the conduct or declarations of the prisoner elsewhere and subsequent to the transaction on Blannerhassett's Island can be admitted; because such testimony, being in its nature merely corroborative and incompetent to prove the overt act in itself, is irrelevant until there be proof of the overt act by two witnesses.

"This opinion does not comprehend the proof by two witnesses that the meeting on Blannerhassett's Island was procured by the prisoner. On that point the court for the present withholds its opinion for reasons which have been already assigned; and as it is understood from the statements made on the part of the prosecution that no such testimony exists. If there be such let it be offered; and the court will decide upon it. The jury have now heard the opinion of the court on the law of the case. They will apply that law to the facts, and will find a verdict of guilty or not guilty as their own consciences may direct."

The next morning Mr. Hay, after counsel for the prosecution had given serious consideration to the opinion of the court, stated that he had neither argument nor evidence to offer to the jury. The jury then retired and after an absence of twenty-five minutes, reported to the court through their foreman, Colonel Carrington, the following verdict endorsed on the indictment:

"We of the jury find that Aaron Burr is not proved to be guilty under the indictment by any evidence submitted to us. We therefore find him not guilty."

Colonel Burr and his counsel objected to entering this form of the verdict on the record. The court at length decided that the verdict should remain on the indictment as found by the jury, and that the record of the proceedings of the court should show simply a verdict of "not guilty." The following day Burr was released from prison on bail.

The trial was now begun on the indictment for high misdemeanor against him, for having set on foot a military expedition against the territory of a foreign prince, to-wit, the Province of Mexico, which was within the empire of the King of Spain, who was at peace with the United States. The trial lasted until the latter part of October when Burr was acquitted.

THE END

Milton Keynes UK
Ingram Content Group UK Ltd.
UKHW030743071024
449371UK00006B/585

9 789362 094988